I0791636

How to kickstart your Equality Diversity & Inclusion journey in six simple steps

SAIDA BELLO

BALBOA.PRESS

A DIVISION OF HAY HOUSE

Copyright © 2024 Saida Bello.

All rights reserved. No part of this book may be used or reproduced by any means, graphic, electronic, or mechanical, including photocopying, recording, taping or by any information storage retrieval system without the written permission of the author except in the case of brief quotations embodied in critical articles and reviews.

Balboa Press books may be ordered through booksellers or by contacting:

Balboa Press
A Division of Hay House
1663 Liberty Drive
Bloomington, IN 47403
www.balboapress.co.uk
UK TFN: 0800 0148647 (Toll Free inside the UK)
UK Local: (02) 0369 56325 (+44 20 3695 6325 from outside the UK)

Because of the dynamic nature of the Internet, any web addresses or links contained in this book may have changed since publication and may no longer be valid. The views expressed in this work are solely those of the author and do not necessarily reflect the views of the publisher, and the publisher hereby disclaims any responsibility for them.

The author of this book does not dispense medical advice or prescribe the use of any technique as a form of treatment for physical, emotional, or medical problems without the advice of a physician, either directly or indirectly. The intent of the author is only to offer information of a general nature to help you in your quest for emotional and spiritual well-being. In the event you use any of the information in this book for yourself, which is your constitutional right, the author and the publisher assume no responsibility for your actions.

Any people depicted in stock imagery provided by Getty Images are models, and such images are being used for illustrative purposes only.
Certain stock imagery © Getty Images.

Print information available on the last page.

ISBN: 978-1-9822-8891-4 (sc)
ISBN: 978-1-9822-8890-7 (e)

Library of Congress Control Number: 2024912907

Balboa Press rev. date: 10/29/2024

Dedication

This book is dedicated to my mum, Mrs Sikiratu Olufunke Bello (nee Tijani) and my dad, Mr Aliu Adebisi Bello. Huge thanks also goes to my two kids Abdul-Jalil Iginla and Jumaymah Iginla and to the rest of my immediate family in Bristol for their love over the years.

To my mentors, teachers, sponsors, friends, connections, followers and other supporters, thank you for your support over the years.

Ms. Saida Bello
Filton, Bristol
19 August 2024

CONTENTS

FOREWORD BY JOHN SIMPSON

Director at Public Service @ Heart
Public Service @ Heart (publicserviceatheart.com)

Saida is a phenomenon. Her personal life journey reflects her courage, determination and intelligence. In this book she draws on her deep well of lived experience to show how, in very practical ways, individuals can make a difference in promoting equality, diversity and inclusion in their organisation.

Saida's journey includes an education that crossed continents, a career that encompassed different professions, and work in a range of contrasting urban settings. Her legal training has given her a keen analytical eye and understanding of how the law can support system change. Her work as an equality, diversity and inclusion consultant is informed by an understanding of how change can be facilitated at individual, team and organisational levels. This powerful combination is deployed through the various case studies set out in this highly readable book.

Saida has overcome adversity in so many ways. Here she describes how she has faced up to racism, low expectations and discrimination in her life. Her response has always been positive and assertive. Be that through taking initiatives and responsibility; building alliances; seeking out allies; showing her passion for change; deepening her understanding of how to facilitate change; using evidence judiciously; developing an indomitable spirit; and sheer hard work.

She is strong on the role of leaders and leadership in role modelling best practice and in leading the development of a wider competence and capability that enables open and productive conversations about matters concerning equality, diversity and inclusion – not least by building a shared intersectional framework for thinking about, and developing, practice. This is combined with an understanding, not least through her work as a professional coach, of the importance of listening, judicious questioning, and the promotion of self-reflection for individual and organisational learning.

Saida shows the importance of a pro-active approach to seeking out professional development opportunities. She illustrates this through the way she has taken part in training programmes, sought out mentors and coaches, identified and undertaken non-executive roles, volunteered to chair groups, read widely, and help build personal and professional networks.

Saida has a tangible passion for promoting equality, diversity and inclusion. She brings authenticity, optimism and hope that things can get better and, in doing so, is a powerful role model herself.

You'll learn a lot more about Saida and her journey by reading this book. You'll also be provoked, through her own case studies, to consider ways you can make your own contribution to making your own organisation, and the wider world, a fairer and more just place.

I've learnt a lot about equality, diversity and inclusion from Saida and am confident that, by reading this book, you will too.

PROLOGUE

Lagos to London – an unexpected journey

I wrote this book to share with other people how I started on my equality, diversity and inclusion (EDI) journey in 2017. It is the story of how a local authority lawyer decided to embark on a journey as an EDI leader. When I first joined LinkedIn, one of our senior leaders in local government said, "local authority lawyers should be seen, not heard", when I asked her whether she was a member of LinkedIn. In other words, we were not supposed to have a public profile and really, we are expected to do what we are told. I ignored my school's career adviser who told me not even to consider a career in law because apparently attending a comprehensive school in Peckham did not put me in the right position. To be fair, becoming a lawyer in the UK was a pipedream for an immigrant who had come from Lagos to London only 8 months before that careers meeting. My dream felt crushed, but I persevered. I went on, not only to become a solicitor, but the senior housing solicitor at the London Borough of Camden, a prestigious local authority and also Birmingham City Council, the largest local authority in Europe. As a senior solicitor at both local authorities, I advised clients on complex homelessness and Supreme Court cases that enabled me to visit the High Court several times and the Supreme Court once. I also managed about 12 members of staff as well as consultants. Not bad for a girl who went to a comprehensive school in Peckham!

Thanks to LinkedIn, I have been able to share a lot of the EDI work I have done with multiple stakeholders from 2018 to date. This continues to lead to many enquiries about how others can get started and what more can be done to make this world a more equitable place.

This book aims to deal with the first question—how to get started and make an impact, fast. In terms of what more can be done, the answer is - a lot. Much more definitely needs to be done to achieve equity in the workplace for minority groups. If we look at recent global incidents, such as Covid-19 and the wars in Ukraine and Gaza, we can see clearly that more needs to be done to ensure that equity, rather than equality, is the order of the day. The nuance between equity and equality is important because the former acknowledges that the starting point is different for everyone. In contrast, equality remains an elusive concept as we will never operate from a level playing field.

This book looks at how you can get started on your EDI journey and identifies six areas that can get you started. There is no mystique or complicated formula and I will show you how to make that journey straightforward and uncomplicated. The old Chinese proverb 'a journey of one thousand miles starts with a single step' may be well used, but it is very true. I have lived the experience myself. Waiting for the perfect moment, or for the leadership team to act, does not work. If you know it has to be done, do it! Be the change agent.

INTRODUCTION

London to Bristol – the journey begins

Think globally about diversity

In March 2020, just as the pandemic hit, I co-founded the Diversity and Inclusion Strategic Network (DISN), with my counterpart in the NHS in Bristol, to keep the momentum on EDI going through the Covid-19 pandemic. At the height of the DISN's activity, global citizens from many disciplines joined us from all over the world, to contribute to our conversations. We hosted monthly webinars throughout the first year of the pandemic and continued to network with the members of the group, a group that is still on LinkedIn now run by another DISN co-founder.

Diversity is as relevant as ever to all aspects of life, business and community. Regardless of what field you work in, you should be aware of the impact of EDI on your community and organisation. I have had people in the construction industry asking me for support with EDI and I've heard from people in Derby, Norway, India and Uganda. The appetite and the will to change, is out there and I am determined to drive it forward. But as we know, EDI is not everyone's cup of tea. I have had colleagues ask me, in my role as EDI lead, "what about me? What if I don't want to be part of a women's group I'm not Black or gay and don't have children? Why should I be forgotten, or my learning and development not prioritised?"

Embrace multiculturalism

I consider myself to be a global diversity and inclusion expert, because I grew up in a very diverse world, with a father working for UNICEF, representing the organisation in five countries over 24 years. I was only three when my dad started work with UNICEF and we moved into the UNICEF compound in Lagos, Nigeria. That was the beginning of my introduction to a diversity of friends from all nations of the world. When I left Nigeria in 1990, to live with Dad and the rest of the family in Sudan, we went to International Schools in both Khartoum and Nairobi and met people from all over the world. It was a great introduction to diversity and it was embedded in me from day one. The universal law of oneness becomes second nature, once you meet so many people from different countries and different religions and realise that essentially, we are all the same.

At fifteen I came to join my two older sisters at school in London, in the United Kingdom, so that we could get a stable education without having to move countries every five years when Dad took a new UN posting. Immediately before coming to the UK, I spent four years in Sudan, where I attended Khartoum American School, a private school funded by UNICEF. Suddenly finding myself in the middle of Peckham in a UK state school well, you can imagine, the contrast was marked. I described this experience to students at the University of Law in my keynote speeches about my legal journey, in 2022 and 2023.

The keynotes were well received. Many students had already experienced the barriers I referenced, even before they left university. For ethnic minority groups, history seems to repeat itself, despite almost 28 years elapsing. Don't get me wrong, a lot has improved but at the same time there is so much more to be done in the EDI space. The starting line is different for everyone. It is not a level playing-field and achieving equity in the UK seems more and more like a fantasy each day.

Socio-economic diversity matters

The support I received in private school was in stark contrast to what I and the other pupils received at Warwick Park School in Peckham. It was worlds apart. Being a born EDI warrior, I felt particularly uncomfortable with teachers at Warwick Park deciding that some pupils' grades should be capped at between C and E.

"That is so unfair," I said so many times, but no one listened. I felt that the school and teachers had already given up on some students and as a result, the students had given up on themselves. The parents had even given up on their own children by allowing such injustice to continue. We didn't think to challenge the school and teachers about the capping of grades even though, amongst us pupils, we did disagree with some of the teachers for enabling such low aspirations in the children they taught. This was in complete contrast with the attitude of teachers in private schools, who were prepared to push you hard, to reach your potential. The consequence, in Peckham and in other schools just like it, was that aspirations were low and university was something that the majority of my classmates at Warwick Park never seriously considered.

Perhaps it was hard for us to imagine a great future ahead for ourselves, when even lunchtime was a struggle on Peckham High Street. There was basically never enough money around. Pre-lunchtime discussions were around establishing if anyone in the group has any money for lunch and if they did, could they kindly share it with their friends?' Some pupils clearly never had money. Those that did, spent it on expensive Nike trainers, which I am pleased to say I could not afford then and have never purchased for myself, even when I could afford them. I bend the rules for my children, but I have never seen any reason to indulge in materialistic acquisitions for myself.

Levelling up London

School conversations included discussions of who was watching the fight after school, to cheer on two misguided pupils looking foolish in the spirit of entertaining themselves in the most inhumane way possible. After watching my first fight, seeing one of the boys I knew get seriously hurt, while my so-called friends, both male and female, laughed, I realised that I would rather watch Home and Away or Neighbours. After that, I just made a swift exit after school. I was not about to hang around watching fights and threats of violence from young boys who had already decided that they did not have a good future ahead of them.

As a result I was a bit of an oddity in my year group. I was already an oddity for arriving at secondary school 4 years late and having to rejoin year 11 in the year we were going to write our GCSEs. I was told off and beaten up a few times for reading a book during lunch break and on the long bus ride. "Who do you think you are?" one of the girls in my group sneered as she snatched my book on a busy red London bus. I was embarrassed.

I tried to persuade others to go to college and university, but I was ridiculed or met with an indifferent shrug. The most heartbreaking excuse I heard at the time was that their parents had persuaded them that it was pointless going to university because they would be denied jobs or opportunities by White people. I decided then that I needed to get as far away from my school environment, as soon as possible. I felt that everyone had given up on the kids. I mention this anomaly because all the talk about levelling up apparently did not include levelling up London. The huge divide between the haves and the have-nots means that even our capital needs levelling up.

Giving back

In my University of Law keynote speeches in 2022 and 2023, I tell the story of the careers adviser whom I told that I wanted to become a lawyer. Although like me she was Black, she looked at me very seriously and said, "The chances of you becoming a lawyer, having been to this school, are very slim and besides which, I don't think anyone will want to take legal advice from a Black person!" I was staggered, although it was probably true in 1994. I can forgive her for that because it was over 25 years ago and in 1994, the data on solicitors from Black and Minority Backgrounds did not look promising. She was right, the odds of me becoming a solicitor, after attending a comprehensive school in Peckham, with no connections and being a recent first-generation migrant to the UK, were very slim indeed. But I was my parents' child and I believed, as they had taught me, that if I worked hard enough and got good enough, then I would succeed. So I stuck to my guns. Luckily I had an inspired English teacher called Mr Brown whose response was, "She had no right to say that to you!" Along with my mother, Mr Brown encouraged me to pursue my dreams, regardless of the environment I was in.

So, I did just that. I completed my secondary education at Warwick Park School on Peckham High Street and went on to Southwark College, Waterloo. I moved to Bristol in 1997. I was accepted to study law at the University of the West of England on clearing, as I didn't make the grade I wanted. One reason I had applied to Bristol and Essex was that I wanted to get out of London, where so many people I knew had the same defeatist mindset that my career officer had. People shook their heads and warned that even if I went to university, I would never get a job, becoming a solicitor was definitely out of the question. I was determined to prove them wrong.

STEP 1

Understand your evidence-base

Be authentic

Simon Sinek explains this idea best: 'Start with your reason why.' We have witnessed countless examples of performative action since the sad demise of George Floyd in 2020. Organisations clamoured to look good and play on the emotions of their staff and stakeholders. But they did not really understand what all the fuss was about. It is not good enough to pay lip-service to the concept of EDI, or to do it only because everyone else is. It is so important that you identify the evidence base for your particular organisation. You need to know why you want to do it and have the evidence to support the action you are taking. A strong evidence base is what will drive the momentum and keep efforts going, long-term. As we have witnessed in the last four years, the organisations that never really understood what the fuss was, have gone back to their old ways. When things got tough (Covid, cost of living, inflation) they decided that EDI was no longer a priority. They were not being genuine and authentic, they were simply following the crowd. That is why their initiatives did not last.

On the subject of inclusive leadership, Bristol chose to be a leader and not a follower. I happened to be working for Bristol City Council three years before the murder of George Floyd. I was fortunate to be able to feed into the five-year 2018 to 2023, EDI Strategy. We were already two years into our EDI journey when the tsunami of social justice, the Black Lives Matter movement, took over the world despite the Covid-19 pandemic. The global social unrest and social justice uprising culminated in the toppling of the statue of an ex-slave trader, Edward Colston, into Bristol Harbour. But fear not, Colston was rescued and restored in the museum in Bristol. His legacy lives on.

Inclusive leadership

In 2016, Marvin Rees had been elected as mayor of Bristol, the first Black elected mayor in the whole of Europe. Some would say it was about time. But some clearly wished they had never seen the day. I started work in Bristol City Council in 2017 as a locum solicitor. I was minding my own business in the legal department when I was approached by an EDI consultant I admire deeply, Simon Nelson.

The senior leadership were engaged in the EDI agenda in Bristol and this undoubtedly made it easier. However, the success of the EDI agenda in Bristol was also due to an alliance with the Bristol One City Partners who supported the agenda. I was proud to say that two huge supporters were law firms, Burges Salmon and Osborne Clarke Solicitors. I became a Director of the Bristol Law Society from 2019 to 2021 to help set up an EDI Committee there too. It was amazing to have so much support from fellow lawyers.

Good role models

We speak a lot about role models and for me, the amount of effort and hard work, a lot of it unpaid, that I put in to drive EDI forward, was in major part due to role models who inspired and motivated me. When things were not going so well, or I met the usual barriers, the greater challenges that my role model, Marvin Rees, was facing, kept me going. He was fortunate to have been supported by a straight-talking, charismatic EDI warrior Queen, Deputy Mayor Asher Craig. Just a glimpse of either of them at the end of a corridor at City Hall would be enough motivation to keep me pushing for equity! In 2017, Bristol City Council was far from diverse and the atmosphere could be described as hostile to difference, whether based on ethnicity, sexuality, disability, or other differences. Staff who had been there for too long, were set in their ways and did not want to see change.

Representation matters

My fellow Bristolian, Aisha Thomas, summed it up nicely: 'Representation matters.' One thing was clear—the evidence. Our evidence base was informed by the lack of representation of minority groups in senior leadership positions across both the City Council and the city as a whole. We knew that the approach had to be city-wide and the Bristol One City Plan, working across all sectors, was the best way forward. A proud moment was definitely the Global Parliament of Mayors event, where the council hosted mayors from over 80 countries all over the world. I got to see Black and Brown mayors and I realised that representation matters.

Bristol Equality Charter 2017

In 2023, when I was asked, at an interview which moment stood out in my EDI journey, I said it was the launch of the Bristol Equality Charter 2018. As always, challenges, barriers and unspeakable things were going on internally. But we had to keep pushing forward for change. The launch of the Bristol Equality Charter was held at the M-Shed, a community hub in Bristol. The charter was significant because it was a city-wide charter that was co-created by Bristol citizens who worked in the private, public and not-for-profit voluntary sector. The aim was to create a more inclusive city of Bristol that was fairer and more accessible and where everybody felt a true sense of belonging. On a personal level, at that launch, it was more about strengthening and empowering individual voices from the ground level. At the time, I was the staff network chair, representing the Black and Minority Ethnic Employee Group (BMEEG).

I remember that the room was crowded, at capacity, with more than 200 people. There was a big board where everyone attending had to sign to pledge their commitment. It was a very emotive moment, partly because dozens of people in the community were involved. It felt as though we had a warm and happy connection to each other. It was a big day, a significant moment.

Our leaders in Bristol had the long-term vision to make the charter a sustainable cross-city effort. When I became chair of an equality and diversity group board, about two years later, I used the charter as a starting point to plan my EDI chair role. This was for the Golden Key Partnership Board, another city-wide initiative. The charter and its eight points turned out to be very helpful in providing me with an outline for the board's EDI strategy. To keep the charter alive, we formed the Bristol Equality Network, of which I was a member. I met quarterly with the other 'change agents' from all sectors in Bristol, private and public, the two universities and not-for-profit organisations.

The Bristol Equality Charter commitments Included gaining an understanding of how representative your work force was and understanding your organisation's evidence base. When you decide that it is time to start your EDI journey, the following can be a great starting point:

- Look at the overall workforce representation of minority groups
- Report on diverse representation in senior roles
- Undertake annual surveys to ask staff about their experience of working for the organisation
- Form a focus group of a dozen or so employees to give their confidential view of working for the organisation, to better understand the organisational culture
- Compare the representation within the organisation with the demographic in the country and the local area
- Look at responses to the staff surveys from different diversity groups, such as LGBT+, young employees voice, disabled employees network, to determine your priorities, etc

I have always been a strong advocate of intersectionality when it comes to the role of staff networks. There are many definitions of intersectionality. To me, in the context of staff networks, intersectionality means the interconnected nature of different protected characteristics. This word has guided my approach to the role of staff networks (also known as employee networks). As the chair of a staff network from 2017 to 2020, I actively encouraged all four staff networks to work closely together. The four staff networks met with senior management collectively to ensure that we had an even greater impact on the organisation.

Lead by example

In order to lead the change by example, I joined the Stepping Up diverse leadership programme as Cohort No. 1 member in January 2018. Stepping Up was created as a direct result of the evidence of the lack of representation of minority groups at a senior leadership level. Because we wanted to recruit people to go on the programme, we advertised across all sectors in the city. The programme allowed people to undergo the training in work. There were six 2-hour leadership workshops and a mentor was provided for six months. We also did a stretch assignment that involved a project that we worked on with our action learning set (groups of six). My set decided to take up the offer to study an MBA in leadership and management, which I completed early in 2022, thanks to Stepping Up programme and the Council's apprenticeship levy. As my MBA was an apprenticeship, I was able to work closely with three different leadership teams on secondment and on a fixed-term contract, which enhanced my apprenticeship.

Celebrating success

The Stepping Up Programme should be celebrated for being forward-thinking and innovative. The programme has sought to tackle the issue of the lack of representation at senior levels, head on. It was backed by Baroness Ruby McGregor-Smith who reviewed race in the workplace in the Race in the workplace report, 2017. Both Baroness McGregor-Smith and Lord Simon Wooley attended the launch of the Stepping Up Programme in January 2018. Fast forward to 2023 and a report was published by the Society of Local Authority Chief Executives and Senior Managers (Solace). The report "Understanding and Improving Equality, Diversity & Inclusion in the Local Government Workforce" found that there was still a lot to be done in relation to EDI in local government, particularly in senior leadership roles. As an associate consultant of Solace, I am determined to play my part in ensuring that EDI remains on the agenda of all local authorities. The lack of representation in senior roles in local government, particularly in London, is simply unacceptable in this day and age.

Stepping Up Rising Star Award in 2021

Stepping Up Ambassador Award in 2022

Stepping Up Cohort 2 graduation in 2020 with the then Chief
Constable of Avon and Somerset Police Andy Marsh

Stepping Up Leadership academy
receiving CIPD awards in 2023

Stepping Up team receiving CIPD award
for the Best EDI initiative in 2023

Case Study 1

The Stepping up leadership programme

I decided to participate in the Stepping Up Programme in 2018. The mayor, Marvin Rees and the deputy mayor, Asher Craig, had decided to launch the programme, as there was a clear evidence base that, across the city of Bristol, the leadership roles were not representative of the communities they served. It was really obvious that this challenge was across all sectors, private, public and not-for-profit. I remember the launch of the Stepping Up Programme, in January 2018 and not knowing what to expect. Lord Simon Wooley was the keynote speaker and in his talk, he showed us a website called 'The Colour of Power'. When I saw that website, I was shocked at the lack of ethnic representation across more than twenty different sectors in the UK. One of the things that made that website particularly powerful was that they used photos and when you are looking at a sea of faces, with just one or two black dots amongst them, the point that representation matters really does hit home. It looks odd that at the higher levels, there isn't more representation. It is a stark reminder that diversity matters. That was one of the things that made me want to use my voice in this space and is what led to me pursuing a career in EDI.

The power of mentoring

My participation in Stepping Up was not the first time I had been on a leadership programme. I had previously been on a Diverse Leadership Programme, in Camden, in 2013. This was established due to the same challenges - lack of representation at the top. At that time in Camden, diverse representation was very low in the senior leadership team, with mainly white men taking the lead roles. I am pleased to say that, thanks to the usual leadership that Camden Council shows, a lot of work has been put in by my counterpart Hanad Mohammed, the Director of EDI. Camden is now one of the London authorities that have significantly improved representation at the top.

When I joined Bristol City Council in 2017, the lack of representation was even more glaring. Having lived in London for 20 years, moving to Bristol brought that disparity into focus much more. This was not helped by the fact that I had served time at Birmingham City Council from 2014 to 2016. Although it was a diverse area of the country, the senior leadership team and the permanent staff did not reflect the community they served. An email was sent round about a D&I champion and naturally, I volunteered to be the first D&I champion in the legal department. Only then did I realise the challenges with EDI. I volunteered in the role for about a year and bought my first EDI book when I was in Birmingham in 2016. I decided then that I wanted to do more to help, to make a difference in the EDI space.

The Power of partnerships

Certainly, one of the things that worked was that the Stepping Up programme in Bristol was a different type of leadership programme, based on a one-city approach. This approach brought together partners from the private, public and non-profit sectors to take collective action. That diversity of thought, due to the cross-sector approach, brought huge benefits, as we could look at challenges and opportunities through a different lens. EDI does not require a 'one size fits all' solution. Each organisation needs to determine what is relevant for them.

I was told a story that very clearly demonstrates how failing to work from your own organisation's unique evidence base can have very dire consequences. The story concerns a company who, having read that they should be making provision for Muslims to observe Friday prayers, called in a firm of consultants who identified the best place for the prayer room and facing the right direction for the users to place their prayer mats. With all that done and a hefty bill for consultation services paid, the management discovered that their workforce contained not a single Muslim worker! Had they consulted the workforce, or looked for evidence of need, this would have become apparent before all that money was spent on something that was not required.

Building networks

One of the reasons that the Stepping Up Programme has been successful is that if you are clear on the reason for any action you take, that action is more likely to succeed. Now in its 7th year and on the 11th Cohort, Stepping Up has inspired the creation of related programmes such as "Horumar" which was created for the Somali community in Bristol. Horumar was co-created by several Stepping Up Alumni members including my fellow mindset coach, Zahra Kosar. Our mutual friend, Kam Govind also led the programme, "Step It Up" for individuals who were not yet in middle management but had aspirations to develop senior leadership skills.

The flagship programme, the Stepping Up Programme is a year-long opportunity that includes mentoring and networking with peers and being part of an action learning set. So far, the programme has developed 800 diverse leaders in six years, which is a great achievement. There are aspirations to roll this type of programme out nationwide and to develop an alumni club for participants.

Your communications plan

Getting Stepping Up off the ground was not easy. A lot of employees at the council asked why the leadership programme was only open to black people. We responded by saying that the programme was open to ethnic minority groups in the first year and in the second year would be widened to all women and people with disabilities. In the third year, it would encompass LGBT+ and all other minority groups. This is the point of having a strong evidence base that, in that case, showed the lack of representation of minority groups in senior roles helped. It is very important that everyone feels included, even the majority group so that you have as much support as possible.

In Bristol, we had a clear and solid evidence base that there were very few black people in senior roles and that is what we worked from – a solid evidence base. In EDI, we always say you must be evidence-based and data-led. To get more people on board, at Bristol City Council, we developed an alumni network to ensure that anyone who felt left out could also contribute to the change.

Recruiting diverse magistrates

Another good example of having a strong evidence base was the approach to recruiting magistrates in Bristol. The representation of ethnic minorities as magistrates was, when we looked at it, less than 5%. It was clear that this had to be addressed. In 2017, Mayor Marvin Rees invited me to speak at an event designed to encourage more diversity in magistrate appointment. I seized the opportunity, talked to prospective applicants and told them my own experience as a Valuation Tribunal England Judge. I also had the pleasure of being interviewed on Ujima Radio alongside Sharon Foster who later became High Sheriff of Bristol. The result of our diversity campaigns was that 33 people from Ethnic Minority groups became magistrates that year. The swearing-in ceremony was an emotional event. I was proud personally, to know at least three magistrates who were on Stepping Up Cohort 1 with me in 2018. The change may be slow, but the evidence showed that it was definitely coming.

STEP 2

Empower all employees

Be a leader

By far the most enjoyable part of my experience as a leader was serving as an EDI champion and staff network chair in 2016 and 2017. At Birmingham City Council, I volunteered as EDI champion and advocated for several staff on disability discrimination (the second blind solicitor I have had the privilege to work with), minority ethnic groups (Polish and Black backgrounds) and gender discrimination. There were a lot of issues to grapple with, including why minority groups were less likely to be on permanent contracts and the disparity in treatment of those staff. I started as the only volunteer, so there was no competition. However, I had the one secret for success, which is passion. I bought a book. I read the book. I Googled for information. I got even more passionate. I spoke to so many people, some anonymously and some who wanted something raised. It took me back to my time at Camden Council and the Black and Minority Ethnic (BAME) mentoring programme that I attended. My EDI journey was, of course, a continuation of the journey that had begun in Camden in 2012 on the subject of representation.

By the time I was appointed as BAME staff network chair at Bristol City Council in 2017, I had already been EDI champion from 2015 to 2016 in Birmingham and an influential voice on Camden BAME programme in 2013. The programme, which was launched for good reason, almost ground to a halt, as BAME staff at Camden thought it was hinting that they weren't capable of doing it all on their own. At a pivotal meeting with about 20 staff, I managed to steer the ship away from a total boycott by BAME staff with huge success, with the majority of participants landing more senior roles within a year of participation, or shortly after.

It didn't occur to me to volunteer as chair of the staff network in Bristol in 2017. The fact that I could be a leader had not registered. I didn't think I had the skills or confidence. It was a complete shock when I was approached by our EDI officer, Simon Nelson, a great man and respected colleague. I was taken aback and surprised at his confidence in me. I will speak more about Simon in Chapter 6, which covers the importance of continuous learning as part of your EDI practice.

Promote grassroots leadership

I thoroughly enjoyed being a member of several staff networks, a chair of one and an advisor to over a dozen others. This role acts as an intermediary between employees and employers, through self-organising groups. It is leadership from the grassroots of the organisation. Our roles and responsibilities included listening to employee complaints, signposting, organising events, writing terms of reference and attending meetings. It is important to know when to signpost employees to HR, the trade unions, or to mental well-being support. I am also a trained well-being champion.

To be effective at signposting, you have to listen, care about employees and not pass the buck. The matters staff have raised to me, as a staff network member or chair, have tended to be around diversity issues such as race, disability, reasonable adjustments, etc.

Hot coffee hot topics with the Mayor of Bristol

In my experience, staff networks can be highly effective at addressing issues such as inclusion, support for working parents, LGBT+ inclusion, young employees and disability inclusion. What these issues have in common is that members of these groups often feel they are in the minority. It is very subjective and it is about how they feel and whether they feel a sense of belonging in the organisation. It is about whether the culture of the organisation encourages diversity and inclusion. We are all human and sometimes when you are in the minority, it is easy to feel excluded, directly or indirectly. Whether or not what people are feeling can be proven, as a leader I believe you must listen to employees and engage in dialogue to create a more inclusive workplace.

The challenges with staff networks

The challenges around how human beings behave, sometimes due to personality disorders, will exist whether or not staff networks are developed within the organisation. The staff networks' existence, in turn, allows open discussion about issues and avoids personality clashes, helping create a great place to work.

The opportunity or space that staff networks enable, create the opportunity to be listened to and valued, which is important to staff. If staff are acknowledged and valued, it enhances their well-being and has an impact on their whole life. Although staff networks do come with the challenges of human behaviour and workplace politics, I would say that the benefits outweigh the challenges. My personal experience, across four different organisations, is that staff networks bring benefits because they enable increased listening and understanding which in turn, improves organisational culture.

Use internal comms to promote the benefits of having staff networks in the workplace:

- Staff networks serve as a reminder to all employees of the importance of inclusion
- They offer the opportunity to hold quarterly meetings to discuss any issues
- They can be a platform to develop diverse leaders, who can serve as ambassadors and model the organisation's values and behaviour
- They can be a good way to signpost staff with problems at work to the right channel (HR, unions, dignity at work or other support) and to represent those who have no one else to support them

- The chance to review new policies, with implications for inclusion, from the employees' perspectives, which will always be different from the employers' perspective (e.g. flexible working policy)
- There is anecdotal evidence that being consulted on issues makes employees feel valued

Create opportunities for dialogue

There are so many ways to listen to your employees that there really is no excuse for organisations not to listen. You can ask them for their feedback in annual or biannual surveys. This will allow them to feel their opinions matter. Employees want employers to take action on the feedback. I worked for an organisation that did not take action on feedback and when I spoke to employees in a focus group to ask why they did not respond to surveys, they confirmed that the employer previously ignored their feedback. This evidence I had unearthed in my initial focus groups was triangulated by the staff survey data, which confirmed that less than a quarter of employees who participated felt like no action would be taken as a result of completing the survey.

I know that some employers and even some HR directors have reservations about undertaking annual surveys because the results are always mixed, but I highly recommend them. When we did annual staff surveys at Bristol City Council from 2017 to 2021, the data showed that things were slowly changing. Employers should not make assumptions about how their employees feel – ask them! This will ensure that they are well-informed when working on corporate initiatives. This will also help avoid low retention rates. Employee feedback is as important as customer feedback. I urge employers and managers to treat employees fairly, because this has a trickle-down effect and it will ensure that employees provide better service to customers too.

Staff networks are a good way to promote the organisation's values and behaviours. When I chaired the BAME network in Bristol, I ordered and handed out cards with our values and behaviours on them. When members of my group made comments that were not appropriate, I reminded them of the values and behaviours of the organisation. I also asked them to demand that their managers abide by the values and behaviours and employee code of conduct. I always informed the chief executives I have worked with, when staff had mentioned to me that they felt that the values and behaviours of the organisation were not being adhered to.

Personal development of employees

Another way I have seen staff networks add value is through supporting the personal development of employees. Quite often, staff from minority groups are not developed at work, due to middle managers not providing them with the support they need. Staff networks can encourage and promote individual learning plans, rather than the corporate agenda. They can run workshops to support employees who wished to move jobs or go on secondment. They can remind the Head of HR to ensure that the performance management systems are fair, inclusive and transparent. They can ask employees to ensure they are having one-to-one meetings, quarterly performance meetings and annual reviews and to ensure discussions are put into writing.

Employee wellbeing

Many diversity and inclusion leaders would agree that staff networks were critical in supporting staff and the workplace environment during the pandemic. At the time the pandemic hit, I was working for the Office for Students and their five staff networks were crucial in holding things together. The articles, the online events and listening circles helped to ensure that staff were positive and still engaged.

A lot of workplace misunderstandings were being resolved as staff networks took an active role. They looked at work/life balance, loneliness, those who still needed to work in the office and those with underlying medical conditions. They offered support with equality impact forms. They came up with health-promotion initiatives, wrote lots of supportive blogs and shared their personal stories. As an EDI lead and a former staff network chair, I could not have been prouder of the staff networks. They thrived because the EDI champion was very engaged and supportive. She even decided to join one of the networks and came to meetings despite her very hectic schedule. Talk about leading by example!

Triangulation of your evidence

The staff networks do not only cover "fluffy" stuff and events, as a colleague once said to me. They can look at reports on EDI before they are published. They can go over statistics and data visualisation and give comments. They are the first to look at ethnicity and gender pay gaps. They are also one of the first in the organisation to look at staff survey results. They usually request the breakdown of the results according to the protected groups, so that we can have more specific ideas about what each group needs. They have brought to our attention real issues, such as talent-management practices. This included the failure of certain groups to progress through the organisation. They have called for or initiated policy reviews, such as recruitment, secondment and talent-management policy.

One of the most effective task and finish groups I co-led was the review of recruitment policy task group. Within three months we reviewed the policy and sub-policies, divided the group into four sub-groups and came up with 36 recommendations for recruitment policy improvement, for HR to then take forward. The task and finish group involved 12 members from across the organisation, including one of the executive team member's Personal Assistant (PA), who became a central and influential part of the task group. We realised that the PA had so much inside information and heard a lot of things and after the first meeting, we could see that she was going to be one of the most important contributors to the project. Always think - is there someone who is not in the room?

Management and leadership

It is important to ensure that management provides support to staff networks and that there is a platform for meetings. We had both an EDI network, where managers and staff meet with leaders every six weeks and a more strategic EDI group for managers only. The structured meetings, with a staff network representative in each meeting, ensure that the staff networks have a forum to speak directly to managers and leaders on the executive team and that access is not just through the EDI lead.

This forum has enabled staff networks to raise the issues they want to prioritise, such as recruitment and career progression. They also came up with new initiatives, such as new staff network groups, events and speakers and analyse the results of staff surveys.

One of the staff network members provided me with feedback, which was that the bi-monthly meeting with senior leaders was the most valuable meeting she attended, as she received direct information about the organisation. In return, staff networks can advise senior leaders of best practice and help increase employee engagement and satisfaction.

External partnerships

Staff networks also provide opportunities to work with external partners and allies. At Bristol, I worked closely with the staff network at Burges Salmon. I spoke at the launch of their staff networks. The seniors leaders at Burges Salmon were incredibly supportive and they provided both resources and a venue for hosting events. I spoke at events about the Power of Staff networks and intersectionality during National Inclusion Week. I also collaborated with colleagues in the NHS such as Sharon Woma, the EDI coordinator and EDI consultant Judeline Nicholas, who later joined us on the leadership team of the D&I Strategic Network which I co-founded in 2020.

Furthermore, staff networks chairs and members are potential future leaders of the organization. For example, in my time as chair of a staff network, I won the Women in Leadership award presented to me by the British Nigeria Law Forum. I also won another award from Bristol University as Bristol's 100 Top Black and Minority Ethnic leaders, alongside the then Mayor of Bristol, Marvin Rees.

Attending event as chair of a staff network in 2018

Winning British Nigeria Law Forum Women
in Leadership Award in 2018

Attending Stepping Up Graduation Ceremony 2019
with my executive coach John Simpson

Attending the launch of the Bristol Equality Charter in 2019
with the Chair of the Young Employees Network

Co-creating an intersectionality workshop with my mentor
Gamiel Yafai and members of our four staff networks in 2019

Organising an intersectionality workshop for staff
networks and stakeholders in Bristol in 2019

Speaking at the launch of Burges Salmons Black and
Minority Ethnic Group Network in 2019

Receiving award from Marvin Rees, Mayor of Bristol

Case Study 2

What do Employee Networks do?

For this case study, I am adding an interview that I gave to Bristol Women's Voice in 2019, as it is still relevant. Huge thanks to my friend, Laura Hillier, for working with me on this interview.

Interviewing Saida Bello, Chair of the BAME Employee Network at Bristol City Council

By Bristol Women's Voice reporter, Laura Hillier

BWV Community Reporter, Laura Hillier, met with Saida Bello, a solicitor working in Legal Services at Bristol City Council. Saida chairs the BAME (Black, Asian and Minority Ethnic) Employee Network at the Council and provided us with an overview of the role of the employee networks in promoting inclusion, equality diversity. Saida has worked as a housing solicitor in social housing for 15 years and is also now working on her 'Senior Leadership Apprenticeship' at the Open University.

Q. What are the Employee Networks?

In June 2018, a report went to senior leaders at the council, which proposed a relaunch and a new structure for the employee networks previously in place. These act to represent the needs and concerns of different employee groups at the council, including the BAME Employee Network, the

LGBT+ Employee Network, the Disabled Employees Group and Young Employees Voice.

The employee networks intend to improve diversity and inclusion in the council. Under the Equality Act 2010, the council has a legal and statutory duty to uphold equality and the employee networks are one way of working towards upholding this law. Membership of these groups by council employees has been increasing, which shows there is keen interest amongst staff in their activities.

Priorities for the employee networks include following up on the recent reports of diversity and inclusion issues at the Council. A key part of this involves providing a space that allows employees to express their views and concerns, which they may have previously felt unable to do.

Q. What do the employee networks do?

Employee networks are working differently this time around. All the groups work together collaboratively on common challenges, meeting every week to discuss how to achieve 32 different goals. A crucial principle and priority underlying the employee networks' task is 'intersectionality' – understanding that people can belong to different groups, which can overlap and interact to result in differing forms of disadvantage.

As many council staff members relate to multiple groups, the employee networks are working together closely, on the same issues. Saida feels that by taking this intersectional approach, the methods of the employee networks are forward-thinking, 'all diversity matters the more we focus on, the better'.

Another significant change to the way the employee networks are working is the frequency of meetings held with senior leaders at the council. For instance, the groups meet with the Head of Human Resources (Mark Williams) every two months, as well as the Head of Paid Service (Mike Jackson,) who has volunteered for the role of Equality Champion every three months. This is hugely positive for Bristol City Council, because 'the best practice for equality and diversity is to get someone at the very top of the organisation to be an Equality Champion'. These connections to senior leaders at the council are also important for the employee networks because concerns by staff can be brought directly to those with leadership responsibility in the relevant areas. As Saida notes, 'having direct access and regular meetings provides an effective channel to tackle these issues.'

All employee networks also have the opportunity to host 'Hot Coffee Hot Topic' events, which are organised by the Mayor's Office. The BAME Employee Network hosted one of these on the 1st of March, which was titled 'How to create a more inclusive culture in Bristol.' The event was open to both internal and external attendees and the high turnout showed that this topic was relevant and of interest to many people. There are also plans for a six-month follow-up event to take place on Friday 27th of September, on the theme of 'Inclusivity/Intersectionality'.

Q. Why is this important for Bristol, as a city?

Unfortunately, Bristol remains an unequal city in many ways, as highlighted in the 2017 Runnymede Trust report into disadvantages and inequalities for ethnic minorities in the city. Saida explains how important it is that work is done to close these gaps, in which having the employee networks plays a part. 'If we empower our staff, they are empowered to do more for the city. If we can deal with the issues now, we're more alert on equality in general and we can intervene sooner.'

The employee networks at the council also have the potential to have a positive influence on other organisations across the city. One idea proposed by the mayor has been to develop an 'Employee Network Charter' with other organisations in Bristol, to support and set the standard for employee networks.

In June this year, a progress report will be taken to senior leadership figures on the achievements so far of the employee networks. This will also contain proposals about what needs to happen next, to keep the momentum going. Saida emphasises that, although it takes a while for systems and cultures to change, 'things are changing and we want the council to be a more inclusive place to work.'

STEP 3

Harness the power of mentoring

Mentoring strengthens mindset

For me, mentoring should be at the core of the EDI agenda. When you are well connected, it is easier for you to find a mentor who will show you the ropes, as your family is likely to have some social capital. Sadly, those from lower socio-economic backgrounds may not be aware of the importance of mentoring, nor have the right contacts that can provide that mentoring.

Through being a member of networks I paid for, I have had formal mentors for between 6 and 12 months. In my experience, the opportunity to learn from a mentor fast-tracks your goals and greatly improves your mindset. My four experiences of mentoring in my professional life have led to me attaining the goals that I set out to achieve. In my EDI career, I went from EDI Officer to Director of EDI within 5 years, thanks to a year's mentoring by Gamiel Yafai, one of the best EDI consultants in the UK. When I started my EDI journey at Bristol in 2017, I commissioned Gamiel Yafai to run two different workshops for me at Bristol City Council. He was a big hit! Due to my excellent experiences of mentoring, I strive to be a great mentor to others and to give back as much as I have received from my mentors.

Ask and you shall receive

When I wanted to get into management in 2007, I contacted the Chartered Institute of Housing, where I was a student member. I asked for a mentor. Ask and you shall receive. It was not long before I was provided with a mentor, a chief executive of a small housing association in London. He was a Black chief executive, Lawrence Stewart, who sadly passed away before his time. He was the first Black chief executive that I ever met and being close to him once a month, for about 9 months, was life-changing and led to me securing a role as a supervisor at Peabody Trust, within a year of the mentoring. His mindset and self-belief were very refreshing. May his soul rest in perfect peace, Amen.

Subsequently, at Camden Council, I was mentored for 12 months by two female assistant chief executives, who were on a job-share. This mentoring relationship with two powerful women was an eye-opener. I had young kids at the time and I felt both guilty and selfish for wanting more, for wanting to climb the ladder. A voice in my head kept asking me, "Shouldn't you be asking for more time to spend with your beautiful kids?". When I met my two female mentors, I found that I could talk to them about childcare issues, about having to give my son Calpol before leaving home that morning and other issues that they had also experienced. I felt I was in very good company and I realised that women *could* have successful careers while raising their children. I saw the challenges and also learnt how to overcome them, one day at a time.

After a few months of mentoring with them and sitting in on executive meetings with over 12 senior leaders, my anxieties and guilt quickly began to dissolve. The mentoring led to me securing a role with the Treasury Solicitors Department, which was the goal I had set for myself. I had previously applied for two roles with the Civil Service. But once I met my two mentors, who had both previously worked for the Civil Service, I realised that I could do it. My mindset had completely shifted. I remember them receiving a time-wise award for the job share in a senior role. I saw the article in the newspaper and I was so proud of them that I cut the story out of the paper and kept it in my folder for many years. It was a huge source of motivation for me. I still have both of them on my LinkedIn, cheering me on as I continue my journey.

Similarly, I was mentored by a senior employment law judge while I worked as a solicitor at Birmingham City Council from 2014 to 2016. I contacted the Law Society to find out how I could do more to support their Equality Diversity and Inclusion agenda. They advised me to join the mentoring scheme they were running. I applied, got through and I was matched with Judge Fiona Monk. I realised I had never met one-to-one with a judge before. I had sat on the board of Central London County Court as a senior solicitor in Bristol. I had also completed Judicial Work Shadowing and sat with judges for over 15 days during working hours, but this was going to be a different experience and it was exactly that.

A relationship with a mentor was priceless. I got to be myself and I got to find out Judge Fiona Monk's story and her humble beginnings. I got to ask all the questions I wanted to ask and I was encouraged to apply for roles on panels and decision-making bodies, to support my long-term desire to become a judge. This mentoring relationship led to me successfully securing a judicial appointment with the Valuation Tribunal England in 2017.

In the EDI sector, I have paid my dues by putting in over 10,000 hours in the last 7 years. Like most people, I started unpaid and worked evenings and weekends. My quick movement through the ranks was also due to mentoring by EDI champions and mentors, such as Gamiel Yafai. I have also had exceptional coaches and consultants, such as Alan Carpenter and John Simpson, who helped me to be more productive as an EDI leader. Whatever you do in life, seeking support from people who have already walked the path will improve your performance tenfold. You can achieve the success that usually takes decades in a shorter period.

Mentor matching

On the Director of the Stepping Up Programme, Christine Bamford's innovative Stepping Up Programme (2018), I also had access to a formal mentoring programme. I had more than 10 mentoring sessions with David Powell, a Senior Partner at Osborne Clarke Solicitors, which led to my successful move from a career as a lawyer to an EDI leader. My mentoring with David was a pivotal moment in my career. My initial goal, when I met him, was to secure a role as a partner in a law firm. I achieved that within three months but realised I didn't want to be a partner in a law firm. Luckily for me, I shared this truth with my mentor, David and he helped me see the light. We discussed what I really wanted to do and I told him that Diversity and Inclusion were my true passion. He fully supported me in following my dreams and being my authentic self. We had so many deep and meaningful conversations, far beyond the remit of the Stepping Up mentoring programme. I did not have the usual constraints in my head battering me with "What will my family and friends say about this? Will they think I am crazy to give up my legal career?" The honesty, openness and space I had with David was so powerful that it led to me making more than one life-changing decision. Some of the decisions had to do with my personal life, including religion and relationships. As a result of this experience, I have volunteered to mentor three other people on the Stepping Up programme and I make an effort to stay in touch with my three mentees. Just as I enjoy receiving a text message or other message from my mentors, I ensure I send a message to check in with my former mentees to let them know that - hey, I've still got your back!

Mentoring networks

I remember that at Bristol our EDI manager, Helen Sinclair-Ross joined the Southwest Mentoring Network led by Hargreaves Lansdowne. Their senior leader Kevin Milwood was a huge supporter of the EDI efforts. I later went on to co-chair the Stepping Up Programme's stakeholder group alongside Kevin. This was to ensure that we kept up with the best practice when it came to mentoring and matching people with the right mentors. As a volunteer for Stepping Up, I have interviewed applicants and matched them with mentors based on their objectives and sometimes based on the sector they wish to branch into. Most of the matches have been excellent because they are based on mentee preferences.

Find your own mentor

If you are not part of a formal professional network, you can still find yourself a mentor. As I described above, I have approached some mentors directly to seek support, as I was not in the sector at the time. I believe that, regardless of where you are in your career, everyone should have a mentor as part of their continuous development. Whether you are a staff network chair, a member, a manager or aspiring manager, a leader or aspiring leader, you should consider getting yourself a mentor, if you have a goal you would like to achieve, either at work or outside work.

When I worked for the Civil Service for three years, I particularly enjoyed attending the Civil Service spot mentoring events. Through participating in the spot mentoring, I was introduced to Bernadette Thompson, who is now working in the NHS. I remember speaking to Rob Neil, another excellent EDI consultant, about my experience of spot mentoring. I had provided spot mentoring to about five participants and I felt it was useful. Rob offered to introduce me to Bernadette, who provided me with a spot mentoring session. The crucial conversation with Bernadette, who had walked the walk, led to me landing my first permanent role as Director of EDI. Harnessing the power of mentoring will literally fast-track your career.

You have seen how I have successfully reaped the rewards of mentoring in my career and fast-tracked my career in a new sector, EDI. Below, I will share my top tips for successfully reaping the rewards of mentoring.

To reap the rewards of mentoring consider the following:

1. **Self-awareness. What are your own top goals and priorities in life and at work?**

   Firstly, ask yourself, what is important to me? What do *I* really want? As a certified coach, I recommend using the 'wheel of life' resource to review your life in your top 12 areas. Then select the one goal you want to work towards and seek a mentor to help you achieve that goal a lot faster than you could do otherwise. For example, I first decided that I would like to become a judge and be involved in making really important decisions, in 2012. At the time, I had only four years of Post-Qualification Experience (PQE) as a lawyer and I knew that usually, judicial roles were open to lawyers with five to ten years PQE. I attended two judicial training courses and applied for at least three roles a year. I didn't secure a single interview in the first four years. Then, in 2016, I set a goal to apply for a role as a judge. This led to me joining the Law Society's mentoring scheme, which matched me with a mentor who was an experienced senior Employment Tribunal judge. From an EDI perspective, diversity in the Judiciary was a goal for the Law Society, so our objectives were aligned. I applied for three judicial roles that year and was successful in securing a judicial post within 12 months of the mentoring.

2. Focus on one goal at a time

Once you have used the wheel of life resource and identified at least 8 of your goals, I would recommend working on only one or two goals at a time, with a mentor. Ideally, you should pick one goal that you are desperate to achieve, so your mentoring sessions are focused. I would recommend writing down exactly what the goal is and looking at that goal each day, as a reminder to reinforce it daily. This is because, as we know, we have so much going on in life. Although I had other goals in the 12 months that I worked with my judicial mentor, no other goal was discussed during our mentoring meetings. After the usual small talk, all we discussed was judicial appointments and applying for quasi-judicial roles, such as a member of a decision-making panel. It is really easy to ask for advice about other areas of your life and to discuss other topics, but to make progress towards your goal and to maximise the time you have with your mentor, I would recommend staying focused on that one desperately desired goal.

3. Decide to get a mentor and fix the date you want to start

I am sure some of you will be thinking, 'So how do I go about getting a mentor?' You can find a mentor by researching mentoring schemes. For example, if you are a member of a professional association, contact their office and advise them that you would like a mentor. If you are not a member of a professional body, then find one that is relevant to the goal you are trying to achieve, join the group and then ask for a mentor. If you are pursuing a personal goal outside of work, join a relevant network, attend a few meetings and then ask for mentoring. Another way I have secured mentors in the past is by asking people in my network, who can mentor me to learn a new skill.

For example, as a housing lawyer, two of my mentors were provided to me free by the Law Society and the Chartered Institute of Housing. I have also been provided with short-term mentors by Solace (the Society of Local Authority Chief Executives) and the Women Lawyers Division of the Law Society. When I joined Solace as a consultant, I was provided with a mentor who showed me the ropes. When I had a specific desire to work as a tribunal judge, the Women's Lawyers Division put me in touch with a tribunal judge who talked me through her role. I have successfully had both formal and informal mentors. Informal mentors are those you go out to lunch with and ask those questions that are best answered in person, rather than on the phone or online meetings.

4. Agree and respect boundaries with mentors

Once you have secured a mentor, it is best to define the nature of the relationship in writing, to ensure that your interactions remain professional. You should ideally agree when you will meet, how frequently, the end date for the mentoring and the dos and don'ts of the mentoring relationship. Find a sample mentoring contract online and aim to follow it, either formally or informally. It is good to remember that the mentor has their own objectives and priorities for the year and they are not agreeing to give you an unlimited share of their precious time. My advice is that the relationship should take place within normal working hours and at agreed times. The Law Society's scheme that I joined contained a very helpful contract that set out both parties' roles and dos and don'ts of mentoring, which was very helpful for me to understand the boundaries.

5. Ask your mentor lots of questions

At every meeting, or in between if he or she has invited you to, ask questions. The greatest benefit of mentoring is that you are being advised and supported by someone who has already achieved what you want to achieve. You have a great opportunity to learn from someone who has already walked the walk. Use it, don't lose it! Ask questions about how they did it and then ask again and again!

Fortunately, my judicial mentor allowed me to email her between meetings, so she had the details of what I had done beforehand. Our meetings were, therefore, a great opportunity to ask numerous questions face-to-face about her role as a judge. How she got there, how she felt at the time, how she fared at interview. Listening to her recount stories of the experience, triumphs and challenges, enabled me to visualise myself achieving those same results. Rubbing shoulders with someone who has done what you want to do helps you imagine yourself having achieved those goals. I started to imagine myself reaching my goal. I went to my interview feeling super confident that I could achieve the goal.

6. Follow your mentor's advice and guidance

My mentor's advice was like gold dust to me and I followed the advice to the letter. I demonstrated this by preparing for each mentoring meeting for at least two hours, to ensure that I had done exactly as my judicial mentor had recommended. I also took the time to type up the action points from all my mentoring sessions, which I then sent to them to check. This showed them how serious I was about my goals. I ensured that I spent at least an hour a week on action points, before meeting the mentor for the next session. This ensured that our one-to-one meetings each month were productive, with previous action points having been achieved.

7. Informal mentors

I have also benefited from having informal mentors such as the Director of Stand Against Race and Injustice, Alex Ardalan-Rakes

MBE and Peaches Golding OBE, His Majesty's Lord-Lieutenant of the County and City of Bristol. Informal mentors can give you advice about anything from attire to wear and what to expect in new or unfamiliar environments.

Celebrating King Charles III
with two of my informal mentors in Bristol

Co-creating an intersectionality workshop with my mentor
Gamiel Yafai and members of our four staff networks in 2019

Featured in the Law Society Gazette in 2017 with my mentor Judge
Fiona Monk who has supported my career development since 2016

Stepping Up programme graduation with Osborne
Clarke and my mentor David Powell

Case study 3

Third time lucky!

In 2017, I made it on the cover of the Law Society Gazette. For a local authority lawyer, being on the cover was like a dream. The article was about the Law Society's mentee making the bench. The cover photo was of me and my mentor, Judge Fiona Monk, sharing our stories about how we got matched on the scheme and how she supported me for a year to achieve my goal.

I had contacted the Law Society to find out more about the diversity agenda. They advised me to join their mentoring programme if I wanted to change things. On the Law Society's Diversity in the Judiciary programme, and as mentioned, I was matched with a judicial mentor, Fiona Monk. We kept in touch after the initial warm-up meeting and I ended up meeting with her every month for a year. At the time she was the Regional Employment Judge in Birmingham. She is now President of a Tribunal. And yet, Judge Fiona Monk is one of the most down-to- earth people you will ever meet.

Within 12 months of being matched with Fiona, I was appointed as a judge. I had applied twice before for the position and failed. She inspired me because she had come from a modest background and worked her way up. She had worked in a law centre and seeing how she had overcome her challenges and succeeded, I realised that there were no limits for me! I used to go on the circuit judging council tax appeals and other issues. Now, however, it is all online! Fiona and I are still in touch and recently she asked me to reverse-mentor her – to teach her what life is like from my perspective.

In 2015, I saw an internal advert to be the diversity and inclusion champion for the Birmingham legal department, the EDI champion. Through that role I soon came to know about a lot of diversity issues within the department. As Birmingham is the largest local authority in Europe, it was a large department with more than 100 lawyers. Unfortunately, however, despite the diversity of the service users, there was a marked lack of diversity in the senior and permanent roles within the legal department. The irony was palpable and although in the lower ranks there was a diverse workforce, they were on fixed-term contracts that lacked security. This was so noticeable that it was becoming a topic for discussion with many staff, which I drew to the attention of management.

I spoke to staff, experienced in such issues and that gave me great insight. As I got more familiar, I knew then that I wanted to follow the path of EDI, because of the type of enquiries I dealt with, which were very diverse and included disability, race and ethnic background. One client, who was partially sighted and a good worker, only needed a taxi to help her in the winter months. It was a struggle to get her the little help that she needed. Then there was another from Eastern Europe who felt she was excluded. One of the saddest cases was a woman who had a history of mental health problems and who was openly laughed at, by fellow lawyers. We became good friends and we kept in touch for eight years after I left Birmingham. The variety was immense and challenging, but I wanted to do it. What intrigued me was that some people did not want to speak up and did not want me to raise issues with management. They just wanted to be listened to. As lawyers, we lead busy lives and we are task-focused, so we do not always make time to ask how colleagues are doing. What I realised, in my role as EDI champion, was that many colleagues just wanted someone who could give them space to be listened to.

Reverse mentoring with Fiona in 2023

Seven years after volunteering to be EDI champion at Birmingham, trying to make a difference to colleagues' lives, the saga continued in the workplace. I was honoured when Fiona, who I had been in touch with since my mentoring in 2016, contacted me to discuss reverse mentoring, which I had championed at Bristol City Council with the employees' network. I believe it fosters better understanding between leaders and staff. When I explained some of my experiences as a Black Woman in the workplace to Fiona, she was surprised. As an overqualified Black Woman with an MBA in local authority, I encounter a lot of micro-aggression and prejudice from managers with insecurities about whether their jobs could be on the line from people like me. I shared some of those experiences with Fiona. I also offered solutions, such as better dialogue and communications, to explain to people why EDI is being prioritised. Some people believe it is a threat to them and are willing to bully, harass and intimidate people in the workplace. The objective was to show that these issues remain live and more must be done to share the challenges and barriers that are experienced by minority groups in the workplace.

STEP 4

Upskill your managers

A game-changer for enhancing EDI in any organisation is upskilling managers who should be upskilled to enhance EDI efforts in the workplace.

As a manager for over seven years, I have had responsibility for up to 12 staff in three different roles. As a board member and a non-executive director, I have sat on more than five different boards and led organisations, including providing expertise of EDI. As a certified coach and a Chartered Institute of Personnel and Development (CIPD) qualified professional, I have been able to add value to organisations by being a great manager of people. I have also successfully managed upwards to drive the EDI agenda forward.

Accidental managers

Unfortunately, in the corporate world, my experience is that most managers find themselves in management roles without having undergone any, or at best just a little management training. Then, once they become managers, they are "too busy" to go for training.

For me, managing people was a privilege from the start. I knew that people like me were less likely to be given the opportunity to manage others. Consequently, I self-funded and attended management training with Shelter before I became a manager. In other words, I had done my homework. I wish more managers would do the same. In 2023, I remember reading an article by the Chartered Management Institute about the deficiency in management skills in most workplaces. I could not agree more.

Continuous development of managers

As I mentioned in the mentoring section, I had sought a mentor through the Chartered Institute of Housing, before I secured a role as a manager. The specific purpose of the mentoring was to secure a management role. I had the privilege of being mentored by a chief executive of a small housing association in Vauxhall (Lawrence Stewart, my first mentor – may his soul rest in peace). I met with Lawrence for one year and then went on maternity leave. Within 18 months of the mentoring, I was in my first supervisory/management job, due to secondment opportunities opening up in my team. I had worked hard to become a manager and sought the skills and guidance on how to manage, from Lawrence. The amount of work I had to put in to secure a management role made me value the role and position of trust I was in. I wish more managers could do more with the privilege. Even after I secured my second opportunity to manage at Camden Council, I continued my development as a manager by completing over 30 training courses at Camden from 2009 to 2014. When I got the opportunity to study for an MBA in in 2018, as part of the Stepping Up programme, I embraced the learning with open arms. I successfully secured my MBA in leadership and management in 2022.

Chartered Management Institute

Unfortunately, my 20-year experience in the public sector corporate environment has shown me that most managers have not taken up additional learning in the skill of management. Many of my counterparts have not had time to undergo any management training. As a manager at Camden Council, I attended just about every single course that Camden HR had on offer. I came to know the people in the Learning and Development (L&D) team at Camden and I have connected with L&D colleagues in almost every organization that I have worked for.

Being a people manager has never been something that I take lightly and I have continuously concentrated on developing myself as an excellent people manager. My management skills led me to the EDI sector because I had noticed that the majority of managers are task-focused rather than people-focused.

I have learnt that the art of management is being able to get things done through other people, through delegating and trusting your staff. In contrast, most of my counterparts have tried to manage by controlling and micro-managing staff, especially when things are going wrong. I believe that the majority of managers I have met in the corporate world have not taken the time to learn what the art of management is. The consequences of this, for people management and the workforce, are dire. I have witnessed high levels of bullying, harassment and race discrimination by managers when things are not going well and they need someone to blame. The truth tends to be that the managers have failed to set any objectives for staff and failed to monitor those results and then they try to discipline or dismiss employees, without following policies and procedures. This will inevitably lead to really high attrition rates and a lack of motivation in the workplace.

Management training should be mandatory

At Camden Council, I stood out as a people manager for religiously undertaking bi-monthly 1-2-1 meetings with staff and for ensuring I always had a 6-weekly meeting with my team. After a while, my team essentially managed itself. I had a highly competent legal secretary and together we ensured that I did not need to micro-manage my staff. I could completely trust my staff and as I gained their trust and respect, everything worked like clockwork.

My staff attendance was high and sickness absence was low because I trusted and valued my staff. I recall that, when we ran the Future Camden 2014 project on hybrid working, successfully implemented six years before Covid-19 hit, my team was the first team in legal to be working from home two days a week. Such was the absolute confidence and trust I placed in my team, that I did not have to check up on anyone.

Management by outcome

So how did I do it? I managed by outcome. I simply set the five objectives at the start of the year. I was transparent about the objectives, my team of 12 knew each other's objectives and we met every six weeks to review them as a team. At my 1-2-1, I concentrated on supporting staff, finding out about family or other issues they wanted to discuss during that private 1-2-1 time and the work took care of itself. I was managing by "outcomes" rather than by presenteeism in the office. Camden's Future Council 2014 project and our move to 5 St Pancras, allowed me to do that. As a new and skilled manager, who had attended all HR courses, I knew that I didn't have to check up on my staff, as I had set objectives and I embraced Camden's performance management cycle. Together with our Future Camden project, I had a clear purpose, which was to allow staff to work flexibly and deliver results. We moved to a purpose-built office and allowed all staff to work from home up to two days a week, because we just didn't have enough space in the new building to accommodate them all.

Managing remotely

The majority of middle managers I worked with did not quickly embrace or welcome this flexible working policy, as they were not clear about how they could monitor the output. Although HR were providing courses to help, they had no time to attend them.

I had embraced flexible working wholeheartedly since 2013. That was seven years before the pandemic hit. The forward-thinking approach supported by our Director of Law and Governance and his peers would mean that when the pandemic hit, organisations such as Camden were already prepared. Management by outcomes ensured that managing remotely was not an issue. It enabled inclusive leadership, as I could support my staff to work when and how they wanted to. As a result, my team were highly productive and I could focus my time as a leader on bringing in funding for new projects, such as tenancy fraud, review of tenancy conditions and complex homelessness and judicial review cases.

Be on Board

As a non-executive director and a school governor for five years, my approach to empowering and trusting staff continued to serve me well. The role of a board member is to provide strategic direction and not be concerned with the day-to-day details. A lot of people have asked me how I have managed to do so much and how I fitted things in. The answer is by delegating, setting direction and trusting those who do the day-to-day tasks, to do their jobs. I have never been and never will be, a micro-manager. I have achieved a lot by setting out clear plans and expectations and supporting others to achieve them.

In my diversity roles, as a priority I have encouraged leaders to upskill managers. At Bristol, when I analysed the nature of the majority of complaints received by staff, it was quite clear that a lot of them were due to poor management skills. I came up with the idea of developing a handbook for managers, almost like a dummy's guide to management. It was based on my good experience of management at Camden, which meant that the role of managers was clear and documented and supported by different training. I had thought long and hard about what exactly could be done and I believed this would be the one thing that would help resolve a lot of issues.

Just before I left Bristol City Council to go on secondment at the Office for Students OfS in 2020, I was pleased that the L&D team had decided to run with this idea and I was privy to early versions of the Manager's Handbook. It literally brought tears to my eyes, as I knew that many managers just did not know any better. They had received little training or support on how to manage people and had no time to invest in their own development, as they had busy jobs. I knew that was the case, as I had been in the same predicament as a lawyer and manager of over 12 staff. The difference with me is that most of my additional learning meant late nights and weekends catching up with work after attending training. It is not easy to work and learn at the same time. You have to be prepared to sacrifice. But the price I paid (extra work in the evenings or weekends) eventually paid off, as my career progressed both at board level and management level. I also enjoyed high job satisfaction in all my roles because I knew that I was adding value to staff I managed and other staff I worked with.

The skill of managing by outcome would, of course, become more important post Covid-19, when staff were working from home. I remember that at Bristol City Council, I wrote more than two dozen letters to managers pleading with them to allow staff to work from home, or flexibly when they had childcare issues, other responsibilities or minor injuries. I wrote these letters with my Staff Network chair hat on. However, before Covid-19, many managers were reluctant mainly due to trust issues. Covid-19 had a huge surprise in store for those managers.

Management post Covid-19

In some ways, Covid-19 has allowed managers to manage by outcome. However, there is a skill gap in this area that needs to be filled and of course, you don't know what you don't know. Managers need to learn to set SMART objectives, monitor the objectives and then manage staff. In doing this, they get to know staff and support them resulting in less absenteeism and other challenges. The great resignation would not have been 'a thing' if managers knew how to better support staff.

I recall that at Camden Council, some of the management training was mandatory, but the majority was not. At Bristol City Council, there was a reluctance to make courses mandatory. However, due to engagement with staff networks, we were able to put together a handbook for managers, to ensure they had their references in one handy document.

Continuous learning

One key lesson I learnt from my MBA studies and EDI journey to date is that you never stop learning. Whether it is about EDI or about employee engagement, I am always learning. My MBA graduation ceremony at the Barbican Centre in the City of London was a proud moment for me. I am grateful to the Open University and to the apprenticeship levy for a first class learning experience. My mum, sister, aunt, niece and work colleague, Micah Mclean, were there to celebrate my success. It has led to me speaking at EDI conferences across the UK to share my experiences with other change agents, leaders and consultants. Continuous learning by all citizens is the key to making real progress in the EDI space. We must all take personal responsibility for our learning and development.

A few tips on what your managers' handbook could include are as follows:

    i.   Performance management (1-2-1, quarterly, bi-annual and annual reviews)

    ii. Fair recruitment and selection

    iii. Managing diversity

    iv. Managing remote teams

    v.   Individual learning plans

    vi. Managing finance

    vii. Managers' checklist

    viii. Organisational policies such as Code of Conduct

    ix. Induction and onboarding

    x.   Continuous learning opportunities for managers

In my opinion, two of the most gaps of managers in the UK is cultural awareness and multiculturalism. The UK riots in August 2024 shows the extent of this problem in the population at large. This demonstrated the lack of genuine tolerance for difference. This should not have happened in such a diverse environment as the UK.

In May 2023, I accepted an invitation from a gentleman, Hadi Brenjekjy of the London Intercultural Academy to speak about multiculturalism at Kensington Town Hall. The London Intercultural Academy which is operated by Al Saihati Intercultural Center is on a global mission to promote multiculturalism. This led to me being a London Intercultural Academy speaker for the second time in Dubai in June 2024. These international speaking events will contribute to EDI being prioritized on the global stage.

Attending the Global Parliament of Mayors in 2018

Attending Al Saihati Award for Intercultual awareness
conference in 2023 with Dr Hala ElMiniawi from Dubai

Receiving an award for Cultural awareness in 2023
demonstrating that EDI needs to be addressed at a Global level

Speaking about the importance of multiculturalism at Kensington
Town Hall in 2023 courtesy of the London Intercultural Center

Case study 4

Managing by outcome

Managers vs Leaders

I have been so fortunate to have been managed by two of the most inclusive leaders of my career while I was undertaking my MBA studies. Both of these leaders worked for the Civil Service and both were, not surprisingly, the nominated EDI champions in their organisations.

My first manager at the OfS was the head of the Strategic Resource Unit. At my interview for the role, advertised as full-time for six months, I explained to her that although I wanted the role, I would like to work part-time so that I could keep my part-time job at Bristol City Council (BCC). I explained that this option would give me job security after finishing the one-year role at the OfS. It was a cheeky request, but I asked anyway. She went away and spoke to her management team and the answer was, yes! As an inclusive manager, she saw it as a win-win situation. You don't get more inclusive than a leader who, at the interview stage, allows you to do a job advertised as full-time, on a part-time basis, because it suits your particular circumstances!

Build trust with employees

My relationship with my OfS manager got better and better each week. I only started the role as internal EDI lead three days before offices were shut down by Covid-19 and yet she handed me my laptop on day one. She wanted to ensure that I could log on to my laptop from home, just in case offices were shut down due to Covid. I couldn't believe that this manager, who had just met me, wanted to give me the option of working from home if the offices were shut down. It was a secondment, so she could have just cancelled the contract.

In contrast, although I had worked for Bristol for 2.5 days a week for three years, my manager there insisted on me coming into the office even on my half day. Working from home was not an option, despite me being a single mum who needed to drop the kids off for breakfast club and pick them up from after school club. There was absolutely no attempt to build relationships or to show compassion or understanding. This meant travelling one hour to BCC and one hour back to do a 2.5-hour shift on Wednesdays. My manager flatly refused to let me work from home, despite the commute. Every request to work from home was met with reluctance and a very awkward vibe, so I just gave up and stopped asking her. This did not stop me from advocating for other people to be allowed flexible working with my chair of the BAME network hat on.

Inspire and engage staff

It was such a revelation working for my new manager at the OfS. Due to the trust she placed in me, I worked hard and achieved so much during my secondment. I passed all my MBA studies at the same time as home-schooling two kids. I felt fully supported. I achieved everything in my job description and we even co-produced an EDI Strategy, which was not in the job description, but we decided to do it to ensure the longevity of the work. This is exactly what managers are meant to do. To inspire, engage and motivate staff.

Manage by outcome

So, what did my manager do right? At the start of the role, we looked at my job description. We agreed on objectives and I was responsible for meeting them. I updated her weekly for an hour and called her whenever I needed to. At the meeting, she checked in with me as a human being.

How are my kids, family and my studies? She showed me that she cared and I reciprocated. It turned out that we had kids of similar age in the same school trust. We were about the same age. She found out about Ramadan and fasting. She had never spoken to anyone who was Muslim and who fasted before, so she was intrigued. I shared my story and she in turn shared Ramadan and what it entails, with her family. It was never only about the work. It was about me as a human being and when I came up against obstacles and barriers at work, she always took my side and supported me. It was hard to find anyone in the organisation who could find anything bad to say about my manager. She was known for being fair and inclusive and carried out her role as EDI lead, authentically.

The most inclusive employer in the UK

If the Civil Service could be judged as an inclusive employer, based on my two experiences of managers in the Civil Service, they would win. My second most inclusive manager was my manager in the Government Actuary's Department (GAD). I had been warned by many colleagues at all levels, who had worked with actuaries, that they would be shy and withdrawn. I decided to go and work for them anyway and I totally lucked out by having one of the best managers in my entire career, a government actuary. I nominated him for two Civil Service awards because he had a reputation across the organisation as a person who was fair and treated everyone with respect. He deserved and earned the role of Equality Champion. He led the EDI function with authenticity and integrity. In my first two weeks of the role, I spoke to over a dozen people and they all said the same thing about this leader.

When I came across challenging people at work and the resistance from HR that many EDI leads are familiar with, he dealt with the situation. He was very understanding and sympathetic and immediately resolved the conflict. As a result, my role as Head of EDI was productive. I had a look at my job description and ensured I provided the service I was brought in to do. I was highly motivated because I had the right manager.

Similar to my OfS manager, he met with me weekly and gave me 30 mins of his time, even though he had a large team of over 30 to manage. In our meetings, we hardly talked about diversity. He just trusted me to do my job once we had agreed my objectives. Instead, like my manager at the OfS, we both talked about our two children and other interesting things. We often only realised, five minutes before our time was up, that we ought to talk about work! Again, I excelled in the role and did more work than I had ever done in my role as a lawyer because I was motivated and managed very well. Who would have thought that the best managers I would have would be at the Civil Service?

Of course, I am not saying that every manager in the Civil Service is like the two I have described above. I have had a short-lived experience in the Civil Service, in 2014, which I decided to end four months later, for reasons that I cannot go into. Once I left the organisation, other colleagues followed. This goes to show that within every organisation we have some good managers and some that require more training and support. How can we ensure we promote role models, like my two managers in the Civil Service and ensure that the days of bullying and harassment being the norm, or tolerated, are put behind us? This question is even more important for public sector employers, who have the Public Sector Equality Duty under the Equality Act 2010.

STEP 5

Raise awareness through EDI learning

I mentioned in Step 2 above about staff networks, that my EDI journey commenced when I was approached by our EDI officer at Bristol City Council, Simon Nelson, a really great man and colleague. Simon reminded me of Martin Luther King. He speaks with great care and thoughtfulness, each word is carefully chosen. He enunciates his words and he always sounds so important and authentic. I had the pleasure of shadowing Simon delivering his excellent unconscious bias training years later, around 2019, before the pandemic hit. We ran a couple of sessions for the surveyors who worked on a separate site from our main office in Bristol City Hall. This was my first real experience of understanding that the culture of an organisation can vary from one department to another. Providing unconscious bias training to over 12 male surveyors, in a male-dominated sector and office, was a huge revelation for me. Watching an expert, Simon, facilitating the sessions and providing them was just such an eye-opener.

Simon is an exceptional trainer and as he spoke and navigated the training session he did his best to explain the standards expected, to our colleagues, I wondered where he had learnt this kind of patience and perfect composure. Perhaps it was through his decades of doing EDI work. The biggest learning point for me was that everyone deals with things, or behaves, according to their worldview. You don't know what you don't know. There were lots of views that were not in line with our diversity and inclusion objectives and that came as a huge shock to me. Your starting point is to look at things from your point of view and worldview. Although I am a lawyer and trained to apply this to my work, I had to take deliberate action to apply the approach of multiple perspectives to my EDI practice. Having mentors like Simon Nelson and Gamiel Yafai helped me achieve this.

I also learnt that targeted training to departments that need more EDI interventions was a valid approach. I witnessed Simon's belief that continuous learning, expert training and a targeted approach could turn things around for colleagues and the organisation. I know that calling on the expertise of people like Simon Nelson could help employers avoid unnecessary employment litigation, by educating more staff about Equality, Diversity and Inclusion. One of the techniques that Simon utilised was to ask colleagues, "What if that person was your wife or your daughter…. would you be happy if a male colleague at work said that to them?" The look on their faces always changed and that question always brought his point home. Do unto others as you want to be done to you. If it would not be ok for your family members, please do not do it to a work colleague. That's simple enough, right?

As a result of shadowing Simon, my interest in EDI learning peaked. I had attended so much training over the years. There was ongoing research from the USA that said that the training did not make a difference and that it had failed to change the workplace in the last 50 years. Fortunately, as an MBA apprentice across local government and the Civil Service, I was fortunate to have been able to study this as part of my qualification. As part of my MBA research project, I considered how to make Equality, Diversity and Inclusion (EDI) mandatory training courses more effective and engaging for an organisation's employees.

The starting point for the research was to peruse secondary data from the annual employee survey about EDI learning. Following feedback from staff, we wanted to take action so that the training we were providing could be improved. For my project, I undertook desktop research about the effectiveness of EDI training courses. This entailed looking at the actual feedback staff gave following our internal EDI training. As with most organisations, some staff reported that the training did not involve discussion and engagement with other people, as it was delivered via a pre-recorded webinar.

As well as looking at the feedback results from the survey, I used primary evidence, from an internal focus group that I designed and conducted with support from my MBA project supervisor, our Head of Learning and Development. As an expert in the L&D sector, she was well-placed to support me in planning and delivering my project. I also devised a questionnaire with the help of my MBA supervisor. I facilitated the focus group and analysed the results with the help of colleagues at the organisation. The main finding was that, whilst it was understood that organisations need to save money and training budgets, at the same time, staff felt that EDI training in particular needed a more 'human touch.' This required discussion and interaction with other staff. The focus group and questionnaire also provided employees with the opportunity to explore different learning styles and their relevance to EDI training. The fact that there are different learning styles, listening, visual, undertaking activity, etc, further reinforced the point about the engagement and connections we need as human beings to embed learning.

The report found that employees at the organisation believed that blended learning and interactive learning which cater for different learning styles, are more effective and engaging. Employees were generally of the view that webinar-based learning, which was the only option currently offered by the organisation 'X' at the time, was less effective and engaging. Learners preferred 'listening events,' an interactive group, or organisational learning. This, it was thought, could be achieved more readily, by working remotely using Microsoft Teams presentations. With the help of the five staff networks, the ideas put forward in the focus group and survey I conducted were quickly implemented. This is why we need staff networks. Grassroots leadership enables ideas to be taken forward in a much more agile way.

My research recommended that staff networks commit to organising more listening events as a way of promoting EDI learning. It was clear to all that more staff attended and engaged with this event when compared with the recorded webinars, which were mandatory but did not have 100%

compliance. We realized that although the national trend was for more recorded webinars, staff much preferred in-person or interactive online learning for EDI. We, therefore, encouraged staff to volunteer, take the initiative and lead the discussions on the topics that mattered to them.

Unconscious bias training

I remember being extremely disappointed when I learned that, in December 2020, the Civil Service had decided to completely scrap their unconscious bias training course. Of course, the story made the papers and there were arguments for and against. The argument for scrapping it was that after the 50 years that the course had been run, there was no evidence that it worked, or that it could rid us all of our bias. It was argued it may even make some people angry enough to be even more biased against minorities.

As chance would have it, in December 2020 I was already writing my research project on EDI learning. I had read the same reports that led to the Civil Service making their decision, which showed me that a report can be interpreted differently, depending on the motives of the reader. My advice was that unconscious bias training would always be needed, whether you call it that or call it "conscious inclusion".

I compare unconscious bias training and other EDI training, to a driving theory test that we need to take before we start driving in the real world. Saying you no longer need theory tests and that the theory will not help when you jump into the car and start to drive, does not ring true. Nor does jumping to the conclusion that there is no evidence that theory tests work. The decision to stop the training is a classic example of making decisions without considering the subject from multiple perspectives. Clearly, the victims of unconscious bias, who report bullying and harassment year on year, would not have agreed that the course should be scrapped.

Unconscious bias training and understanding the fundamentals about bias (such as the Havard Implicit Association Test), are clearly needed. For example, if you have a good appreciation of learning styles, then you will know that people learn in different ways. Unconscious bias training encourages reflection on where you are with recognising your own bias, is part of the learning process. Of course, this is not going to cure individuals and organisations from discrimination, but it offers a solid foundation from which to assess and reflect on where you are and then, through awareness, you can practice and develop your skills. For this reason, I cannot agree with the Civil Service decision to scrap the course, particularly with no plan for any alternative. Instead of listening solely to the views of academics, they should have asked a few people from minority backgrounds for their views. After all, they are the people who have to live with the consequences of unconscious bias, discrimination and micro-aggressions on a daily basis.

Blended learning

A more measured approach to the unconscious bias training dilemma would have been to review the unconscious bias courses (both content and mode of delivery) and consider how effective the courses are. We all know that there are many mandatory courses that you are required to attend at work that you could quickly click through to get to the end. If you enable your organisation to tick the box and move on, they will most likely not even remember what the course is about. If organisations want to save money, they could do that and engage staff. An option would be to ensure that unconscious bias training requires more engaging blended learning and that we improve the evaluation of training.

Everyone is unique. Everyone is different and has been raised differently. As a result they have their worldviews. If we are going to work together in organisations or get on in communities, it would be good to have a common starting point and shared understanding. Unconscious bias training is one of the ways we can start to do that. A mandatory unconscious bias training course would ensure each organisation had a baseline understanding of what respecting differences and embracing inclusion look like.

Reviewing your EDI training needs

In the Civil Service we undertook regular skills gap analysis before commissioning training. To find out where you are with EDI training you can consider the following:

I.   Which EDI courses do you currently have?

II.   Ask staff to complete surveys about the EDI courses currently on offer.

III.   Ask staff to evaluate the training and how effective it was.

IV.   Ensure your EDI learning offer covers core areas, such as unconscious bias, Equality Act, diversity groups and developing staff networks.

V.   Use mixed learning approaches, such as workshops, focus groups, team meetings and questionnaires to ensure employee engagement.

VI.   Working with sector and industry groups by attending EDI conferences and roundtables.

VII.   Work with consultants who are up-to-date and familiar with best practices in EDI

Attending MBA Graduation ceremony in the
City of London in 2022

Graduation day at the Barbican Centre
with my mum and family 2022

Attending EDI conference to continue to support staff networks and culture change across the United Kingdom in 2023

Case Study 5

Inclusive leadership training

In every one of my Equality, Diversity and Inclusion roles, I frequently come up against the frustrating challenge of persuading senior leaders to attend EDI training. They are invariably too busy to attend training courses, especially EDI training. Finance, budgets, emergencies and almost anything else is, apparently, far more pressing.

Now it is not that I am unsympathetic, in fact, I am very sympathetic to senior leaders, as I know the challenges of finding gaps in their diary. As an MBA student from 2018 to 2022, I had the unique opportunity to shadow and work with three senior leadership teams. I have spoken to so many Personal Assistants (PAs) who struggle to find a 30-minute gap in their bosses' diary. I remember asking one PA whether her boss even got a lunch break! Most of the time, these CEOs work very long hours and grab a 30-minute lunch break, if they are lucky.

One focus group I was on took nine months to organise and even then, only 12 of the 18 could attend. Post-Covid, things are different and I believe that we have to capitalise on what we learned – that not everything has to be face-to-face. Training can be done remotely and recorded so that others can watch it later.

In my EDI role, I had four different meetings and discussions about unconscious bias training over 18 months. I asked so many times for the CEO and senior leaders to attend the training, to no avail. I was frustrated and over Christmas that year I decided that once I got back to work, I would just book the training and invite everyone and I would not ask permission first, either!

I knew it was not within my control whether those invited attended or not. But I did know that if they attended the training, they would learn what bias is and perhaps begin to see things from the perspective of minority groups. I was convinced that our senior leaders were good people who would think differently if they opened their minds to education about unconscious bias. I genuinely believe that the bias shown is mainly unconscious, because, as human beings, a lot of our actions are unconscious.

Even now, I don't know whether it was courage, foolishness, or desperation that made me do it, although I suspect that it was probably the latter!

After Christmas and New Year break, I switched my laptop on and booked an in-house facilitated unconscious bias training session for 16 colleagues, with none other than Simon Nelson. I invited a mix of staff network chairs, the head of HR, other colleagues with whom I was working on EDI and of course, our Chief Executive Officer (CEO). I had become so frustrated about selling the benefits of unconscious bias training to our CEO and other leaders.

Immediately I sent the invite, the head of HR wrote to me and said he would attend but told me in no uncertain terms that the CEO would not attend. On the day of the training, as all the delegates walked in, he came up to me and said, "Well Saida, I did tell you the CEO would never attend. CEOs only ever attend training courses with other CEOs and should not be invited to mixed training sessions. They never attend training courses with staff and certainly not with staff networks!"

"In fact," I said, "when I worked for Peabody Trust from 2005, Steven Howlett, the then CEO of Peabody Trust, attended training courses with staff. I was lucky enough to have sat next to the CEO at one of our values and behaviour training courses."

Just a few minutes after I made the comment, our CEO walked into the training, unannounced! Everyone was stunned – I was stunned! He came in and took off his tie, unbuttoned his shirt and relaxed. Perhaps he had come from a more formal meeting. I went straight up to him and thanked him for coming and then asked the trainer to start. I was far too stunned do any more than that. I guess my own unconscious bias meant that I had convinced myself that he wasn't going to come!

I gained so much respect for the CEO on that day. I never knew why he attended and what he thought of my bold action. Did he think I didn't know my place, thinking I could invite a CEO to an unconscious bias training? In my defence, I felt that my move had come after months of discussions about the benefits of unconscious bias training and my motivation was the thought that, rather than analysing and overanalysing, why not get the CEO and other senior leaders to go on the course and see for themselves?

My respect for the CEO doubled when, at the end of the training, he advised that he had never been to this kind of training before and that he had found it useful. My respect trebled when I was told by colleagues that later he decided the course would be mandatory for his top team of 16!

The moral of the story is that sometimes you just have to back yourself, take the initiative, take risks, be brave, bold, courageous and keep an open mind. There was nothing I could physically do to make the CEO attend the meeting if he didn't want to. He made his own decision. All I did was chip away at various meetings and try to make him see things from a minority group's perspective and have hope, faith and an open mind that he just might come along. And he did!

That little leap of faith was a decisive factor in my decision to pursue a second career in Equality, Diversity and Inclusion. I know now that you need faith that you can find an ally, even when you are not really expecting it and all you have is literally hope and faith in humanity. Sometimes faith is all you need.

STEP 6

Develop your EDI strategy

An EDI strategy does not have to be a complicated document. Thinking that it might be is undoubtedly off-putting to many people. It can be between five and ten pages, but it should be in writing because everything worthwhile needs to be written down. This simple plan of action should be linked to the organisation's mission and purpose. It will help to align you with your corporate objectives through an EDI lens. It should be integrated with the business plan and it should be a plan that can help you to implement your strategies, communicate your plans to staff and stakeholders and show clear commitment. One of the reasons that organisations need a written and formal EDI strategy is that EDI involves the integration of different disciplines. For example, in your EDI strategy you would need to include or cross-reference your approach to the following:

- change-management principles
- project-management principles
- communications plan
- EDI data
- HR workforce data
- inclusive leadership
- EDI learning

Many people think that if they have a plan in their head, that will do, but it really won't! Things might be forgotten and having an actual document shows that you are willing to be held to account. Running an organisation involves prioritising and dealing with multiple demands. A written strategy will help you keep on track with the commitments you have made. Most importantly, it will prompt you to act on those commitments.

The benefits for the leadership team will be:

- To build trust with the staff
- To follow through with promises
- To demonstrate sustainability in all spheres
- To show progressive mind set
- To demonstrate accountability

The benefits for staff will be:

- Feeling more valued
- Feeling secure in terms of psychological safety
- Feeling connected to colleagues and the organisation
- Feeling a sense of pride in working for a proactive organisation

The EDI Strategy should include initiatives to strengthen both diversity and inclusion. While diversity is about the workforce data that shows the differences in the organisation, inclusion is more about conscious steps that can be taken to ensure that staff feel more included. Having a written strategy will ensure that all the areas needed are covered in your plan.

Quite a few companies will say that they will implement EDI from day one. That is like saying you are going to drive off down the motorway without a single driving lesson. Preparation and a staged approach, are the only way to realistically achieve true EDI. The desire to save money is undoubtedly behind this rush to implement what has not even been established. A lack of understanding of what EDI really means is behind this and this is what needs to be addressed.

Research by McKenzie & Company (2020) has clearly indicated that diversity and inclusion lead to greater productivity, creativity and innovation. It just makes better business sense and if you pay proper attention to something, it will work. Filing of tax or annual reports will be carefully completed by companies every year, without fail. EDI needs to have the same attention paid to it.

There have been huge changes to the way that we live and work, since the pandemic. To retain employees, organisations must do more to create inclusive cultures, connect with their staff and also provide career progression opportunities. Post Covid-19, retention has become an even more serious and pressing issue for companies. The cost of recruitment and the first six months training, is expensive and employees leave quickly if the culture of the organisation is not right. In HR terms, we have witnessed what is known as 'The Great Resignation' post-pandemic. The hospitality industry knows about this better than most. They let people go during the pandemic and now they want them back, but in the interim, they have found other work to do and often have had bad experiences with their old employers that would not make them in any hurry to return to work in hospitality.

The onus is now on organisations to adopt practices that will enable them to retain staff because the cost of not doing so means that money and time will be lost, as well as good people. It costs a lot to take someone on and train them, so active steps to ensure staff retention is the first move anyone can make to save organisations money.

Listen and take action

Sending out staff surveys is good, but no use at all if organisations take no action on the points made by staff. The correct way to address staff comments is to reply with what steps are being taken to address their concerns. When people are not listened to, they will get fed up and leave. They will feel undervalued and lose trust in their employers.

I recorded an EDI webinar for the Bristol Law Society, in January 2021, showing how easy it is to put together an EDI strategy. I have spoken in the past to several organisations in Bristol who never did devise a strategy and as a result, were unable to follow through on their EDI ambitions and aspirations. Without anything in writing and with no clear plan, it was more like wishful thinking on their part, rather than a real desire to affect change.

At Bristol City Council in 2018, I experienced the benefits of having a written strategy to keep me accountable regarding what I was working towards in terms of delivery and managing conflicting priorities.

The Chartered Institute of Personnel and Development recommend a written EDI strategy as part of people management. As a member of CIPD, I am convinced that this is the right approach. A strategy can be used by leaders and staff to co-create a more inclusive environment. Having a written EDI strategy can move an organisation beyond diversity to inclusion, but only as part of a deliberate and conscious action by all staff.

A key part of my approach to developing strategy is facilitating focus groups and seeking input from staff to feed into strategy. It is not sufficient to undertake staff surveys without digging into the results using interviews and focus groups. I have had the opportunity to use this approach at Bristol City Council, the Office for Students, the Government Actuary's Department and as the Director of Equality, Diversity and Inclusion at the City of London Corporation.

Stepping Up alumni supporting the Mayor
of Bristols One City Plan in 2019

Facilitating focus groups with EDI consultant Rob Neil in 2021

Taking a selfie with leadership consultant Dion Johnson who was a huge source of inspiration to me at the start of my EDI journey

Case Study 6

Leading EDI on the board of the Golden Key partnership

Over the last five years, I have developed and fed into four different EDI strategies, both as an employee and a board member. I am going to talk about my role in developing the EDI strategy on the Golden Key partnership board.

In March 2019, I was recommended by the then Mayor of Bristol City Council, Marvin Rees, to sit on the board of the partnership. This was an £8m project funded by the National Lottery. Because of my passion for EDI, I was appointed as chair of the EDI committee with about 10 members.

We started with a review of what we were already doing in the partnership organisation in terms of EDI, Golden Key. Using the Bristol Equality Charter as a guide, we started by looking at our staff and service users, from a diversity standpoint. The point of the project was to support people with multiple disadvantages in Bristol. This included people who had been in contact with the Criminal Justice System, the homeless, those with mental health issues and people with drug addiction.

We looked at data on how representative our staff and service-user groups were. What we found out was that our partnership, aimed at supporting vulnerable people, did not have a diverse workforce or clientele. We did not adequately represent 20% of the Bristol population who were from a minority background. We tried to explain why minority groups did not use our services. We were curious to find out where those groups went, for support, if they were not using our services. We later invited people with lived experience to sit on the board of the Golden Key partnership, so we could hear different voices.

Reviewing our data showed that we needed to do something to make ourselves more diverse and representative. We found that because there was no joined-up thinking, along with repetitive form filling and explanations, it was challenging for service users to get a holistic service. We had representatives from all services and we realised we needed to join up the approach to service users.

By the time Covid 19 hit the UK, we had a platform on which services were joined up. In response to the Covid 19 crisis The Golden Key partnership led in removing all homeless people from the streets. This would not have been possible if we had not progressed with the joined-up approach that the Golden Key partnership was designed to promote. The EDI group that I chaired had a similar joined-up working approach, in that we looked at what each organisation was doing in terms of EDI and shared best practice, reporting to the board on our findings.

We still had challenges with representation, but the work we did enabled us to get feedback from representatives of some of the vulnerable people to whom we were offering services. For example, when homeless people were placed in hotels during the pandemic, we could get early feedback about the loss of network for those homeless people, who had been accustomed to living on the streets. They felt cut off from their 'street' community. As a result, we found ways to ensure that they still felt supported.

On the EDI committee that I led, we did a review first and then put together our vision in terms of having an inclusive organisation. Subsequently, we drafted an EDI strategy for the partnership, so that we knew what we wanted to cover in the lifetime of the strategy. We committed to what we were aiming for with our strategy, we had a clear vision and reported every quarter so that we could see we were on track.

It was also critical to communicate what we were doing to increase the visibility of the work. You could be doing the best thing in the world, but if no one knows, then it is useless. There is also the fact that without communication, best practice cannot be shared. The core work of EDI is about influencing behaviour change and we are leading by example, trying to influence others to follow. To this end, we organised workshops, panel sessions and webinars to communicate both with staff and wider stakeholders.

What was the impact?

The impact included better joined-up thinking. This was illustrated by the steps the Golden Key partnership took to help remove homeless people from the streets of Bristol. The pace of achieving the move was a good example of the One-City approach. Linked to that is the fact that the Golden Key Partnership was centred around the systems thinking approach. This meant that everyone tackled the problem together, to ensure the service users could have their challenges dealt with in one place. The benefit for the service user was the 'My Team Around Me' way of getting help, which meant that, as far as possible, they get access to services in one place, rather than having to go to different places to receive different services. This approach was carried forward by the Changing Futures project, which lasted for a further two years.

Equality Impact Assessments

Another significant impact, from an equalities perspective, was that from June 2020 we successfully revived the use of equality impact assessment forms. Under the Equality Act, 2010, organisations, particularly in the public sector, were encouraged to consider the impact of their decisions and policies on the different diversity groups they served. The EDI committee were able to revive the use of the form within the partnership group. Once we started using it in the lead organisation, we encouraged the rest of the partnership to use the form, sharing this really helpful best practice tool.

The Contribution of Lived Experience

We invited people with lived experience to join the EDI committee so that we could get real feedback in real-time. We call this the 'feedback loop.' It helped, as those people, with their lived experience, could put us right and show us how the things we proposed would not work or could work better. Their input was invaluable.

By far the greatest impact of the EDI committee was the fact that a new £3m 'Changing Futures' project has been funded by the Department for Levelling Up. This was centred around this EDI principle, showing the importance of having an EDI lens on any project, along with the deliberate and precise approach of the Golden Key project that has carried forward to the 'Changing Futures' project.

CONCLUSION

From Bristol to the City of London & beyond

I have come a long way since 1997, when I arrived at the University of West of England, Bristol, to study Law. At UWE, I found myself one of only two Black students on my course. We had a couple of Asian students on the course and we stuck to each other like glue. At the University of Bristol there were only two Black students in my Legal Practice cohort in 2000 to 2001. One Black, one Asian. I could not help asking myself, 'Why am I doing this?' It was not fun being the first. It seemed that everything was stacked against me, as there was no one like me visible. But I soldiered on, despite feeling completely out of place. I threw myself into the work and all the challenges, both visible and hidden.

After University in 2001, I wrote 400 applications to law firms to break into the legal profession through commercial practices. Back then I was so broke, that my mother even had to give me money for the stamps. Half of the law firms did not even reply! Back then, in the UK, you had to get a training contract before you could be a qualified solicitor, so it took six years for me to finally qualify, while less qualified and motivated, but better-connected, fellow students breezed into law firms the minute they left university, courtesy of family connections.

While I continued to apply for training contracts, I started work as a legal assistant and because I was good and worked hard, I was promoted and eventually got my own office and caseload. In truth, I had a caseload from day one, but without the payment to go with it! At that time, it was very much who you knew rather than what you knew. The office was diverse because it was in London, but the best jobs and opportunities always went to people who sounded like they had attended private schools, who were assumed to have superior social standing, or whose parents knew somebody in high places! It was always the subject of many conversations but we accepted that there was nothing we could do about it.

I went on to qualify as a solicitor, a week before the birth of my first child in 2008. Five years later than anticipated. I could only afford six months of maternity leave. I could not afford to be on less income, so I went back to work. I went on to excel as a legal manager in local government in Camden and Birmingham and as a locum solicitor and D&I agent in Bristol. I have to confess subsequently to suffering from imposter syndrome, a lot of the time, due to not seeing enough people like me in the legal world in the 25 years that this time covered.

Climbing the ladder

In 2013, I was on the Camden Black and Minority Ethnic (BAME) mentoring programme, mentored by two assistant chief executives. The programme had been created due to a lack of senior leaders from diverse backgrounds in the organisation at that time and it led to me securing a role in the Civil Service.

In 2014, I served as Diversity and Inclusion champion in the legal department of Birmingham. I started to realise that the challenges were not mine alone. They were systemic and the system did not favour people like me.

From that awakening, I kept my eyes open for opportunities to network with people who could help. I am proud to say that I have 10 years' experience in the EDI sector. This experience and my participation on Camden's BAME mentoring programme in 2013, got me to think about EDI issues and the lack of representation of Black and Minority groups and other protected groups, at senior levels of organisations. The programme was a success and the majority of participants either got a promotion or left the organization to secure a promotion.

An ongoing EDI challenge is how to refer to people from minority ethnic groups. I have chosen to use Black and Minority Ethnic (BAME) as my interview in the earlier chapter about Staff Networks uses the acronym BAME. This was still politically correct at the time the article was written in 2018 and BAME still resonates with me today.

One of the most rewarding aspects of my EDI career to date has been my involvement in grassroots leadership as a Staff Network chair. I chaired a Staff Network for over 2 years, and I participated in the inaugural Cohort of the Stepping Up Leadership programme. This gave me the opportunity to feed into projects such as developing the Bristol Equality Charter, developing an EDI Strategy and developing Staff Networks.

I have also worked as internal EDI lead at the Office for Students and Head of EDI in the Government Actuary's Department and Director of EDI at the City of London Corporation.

I feel that hard-won as it has been, progress is being made on the EDI agenda. I am really proud to be a member of the Law Society for the progress we have made in that profession. I have sat on boards (although none were representative of minority groups), I sit as a Valuation Tribunal Judge, which is also not representative of the community it serves.

To contribute to progress on the EDI agenda, I have mentored four people on the Stepping Up programme. I find mentoring to be invaluable because I have been mentored four times in year-long programmes. I have been able to achieve the goals I set before the mentoring relationship began. I feel strongly that mentoring is one intervention that helps bridge the socio-economic divide. I decided to take a break from practising law and to put some focused energy into the EDI agenda and make an impact on a more national level. This book sets out what I have learnt about EDI since I volunteered to be the EDI champion in the legal department at Birmingham City Council. My experience has included volunteering as an EDI champion, being a paid EDI member of staff, an EDI lead, Head of EDI and Director of EDI. The sectors I have covered included local government, the Civil Service and volunteering in the community as an EDI board member. This has therefore included looking at EDI at a strategic level, as well as developing EDI action plans, which enable us to implement programmes and organise events that help to engage employees across the organisation and collaborate externally with other stakeholders.

EDI: Are we there yet?

No, we are not even close.

More needs to be done, senior leaders need coaching and reverse mentoring to begin to understand the perspectives of people from minority groups. Incidents of abuse of power, injustice and inequity seem to be on the rise, which gives power to power-hungry leaders.

More needs to be done to diversify boards, because groupthink prevents companies from working efficiently and delivering services and effectively scanning the horizon to ensure survival.

If we look at recent events in Ukraine and Palestine, we can truly see that the quest for equity, inclusion and diversity is far from over.

In my EDI campfire keynote at the City of London in 2023, I spoke about the importance of emotional intelligence at the top. There needs to be a shift from the business case to the human case. With the growth of Artificial Intelligence, we need to shift towards emotional intelligence and what makes us human, more than ever. The EDI saga continues both locally and globally.

Giving keynote speech on the importance of emotional
intelligence in the EDI space 2023

Conclusion - Telling my EDI story at the City of London event in
2023 organised by Eve Novikova and Elizabeth Garcia Braga-Nieh

My EDI journey continues with encouraging C-Suite to put emotional intelligence at the heart of their People Strategy

ABOUT THE AUTHOR

Ms. Saida Bello, MBA CMgr FCMI
Director of Bello Coaching & Consulting Ltd, Bristol

Saida Bello is the Director of Bello Coaching & Consulting Limited (BCCL) in Bristol. She has previously worked as Director of Equality, Diversity and Inclusion (EDI) and Head of Diversity and Inclusion and EDI lead in the public sector for over five years. Saida is a consultant Housing Solicitor with over 15 years legal experience.

Saida was the Equality Champion in Birmingham City Council's legal department from 2015 to 2016. She contributed to the development of the diversity and inclusion strategy at Bristol City Council from 2017 to 2020. She was seconded to the Office for Students from 2020 to 2021 as an EDI adviser. Subsequently she worked as the Head of Diversity and Inclusion in the Government Actuary's Department and Director of EDI at the City of London Corporation.

Outside of work, Saida has gained over 11 years' strategic leadership experience through sitting on several non-executive management boards. She chaired the EDI steering group on the board of the Golden Key partnership board in Bristol for over three years.

Saida was a Non-Executive Director of Ashley Community Housing, a specialist housing association for refugees with offices in Bristol,

Birmingham, and Wolverhampton from 2019 to 2022. She is currently a Trustee of Quartet Community Foundation in Bristol.

She was appointed by the Judicial Appointments Commission as a Valuation Tribunal England (VTE) Judicial member in 2017. She was appointed as a Chairwoman of the tribunal in 2020. She sits voluntarily as a VTE Judge at least once a month. Her role as a Chair of the VTE involves making decisions in council tax reduction appeals, council tax banding appeals, business rates and other miscellaneous cases.

Saida is a certified European Mentoring and Coaching Council (EMCC) coach and a certified MOE (Me, Others and Everyone) coach with over 13 years' management experience. She is a member of the Chartered Institute of Personnel Development (CIPD).

Saida is a mindset and personal development coach with Proctor Gallagher Institute whose registered office is in Arizona, USA.

www.ingramcontent.com/pod-product-compliance
Lightning Source LLC
Chambersburg PA
CBHW031412250726
48656CB00002B/649